I AM
Stained
Glass

Vision Board:
The Old-School Method
The Good and
the Story of a Hippo

The old-school vision board
is a blast from the past.

It's typically made of a poster or cork board
where you can paste images, quotes, and
affirmations that reflect your aspirations.

The Good

By creating a vision board,
you are setting your intentions
and focusing your energy on
what you want to **attract** into your life.

It can be a fun and engaging activity
that helps you **clarify** your goals
and stay motivated to pursue them.

Many people find that their vision board
becomes a **powerful** reminder
of what they want to achieve,
and a source of **inspiration**
when they feel discouraged or stuck.

The Story of a Hippo

Picture this: strolling through a room and
catching a **glimpse** of your vision board.
But let's be real, after a while, it just
blends into the background like furniture.
The board is **stuck** in a time warp,
unable to grow or change.

**It's like trying to fit a hippo into a
Mini Cooper - cramped and uncomfortable!**

How can we expect to unleash our
creativity with such limited space?
It's time to **break free** and give
our visions the room they deserve!

**Now, get ready to flip the script and
discover the hottest new technique!**

What's Trending?
Pocket Vision!
Your Vision Board Journal

We take the old-school method and make it
POWERFUL!

[The Hippo is out of the Mini Cooper
and he has room to roam.]

Imagine having your
personal dreams and affirmations
right at your **fingertips**, all day long!

You can access them anytime, anywhere,
and give yourself a little **boost**
when you **need** it most.

Convenience is what we crave and
this is as **EASY** as it gets!

Skyrocket into the future with Pocket Vision.

Pocket Vision is a **CREATIVE** tool
that gives you a **personal artist's canvas**
where you can splash your dreams and goals.

It's a **physical tangible reminder**
that you're a **CHAMPION**
and can conquer anything.

Aiming for that dream job, a super healthy
lifestyle, or a happy relationship?
Need a pick-me-up?

Just take a peek at your
Pocket Vision and watch your
MOTIVATION SOAR.

When you feel a bit blue,
your Pocket Vision will be there
to remind you of your **ultimate vision**
and **boost your inspiration**.

It's like talking to a **BEST FRIEND**
that will tell you how loved and valued you are.

Your affirmations will play, like a **favorite song**,
on a **loop** in your head.

When negative thoughts
try to rain on your parade,
Pocket Vision will be there to
kick them to the curb.

With Pocket Vision,
you can **turn your dreams into reality**
by visualizing them and taking
ACTION towards them.

The impact on your life will be
directly related to how much you read and
focus on your vision!

It's the ultimate **UPGRADE**
to your vision board game!

I am inspired!

"Words are Powerful.
Be careful what you write.
You just might get it!"

Michelle Marie

The Power of a Vision Board Journal: My Story

Listen up because
I've got a **MISSION** to share!

As a proud single Mom of 3 and Nana of 3,
I know firsthand how easy it is to
forget our **dreams**, our **worth**, and our **goals**
when life gets chaotic.

That's why I'm here to help you stay **focused** and
reach your **highest potential** with some daily
reminders of your **awesomeness**!

I know what it's like to be the rock of the family, to
provide for everyone,
and to feel like you're running on empty.

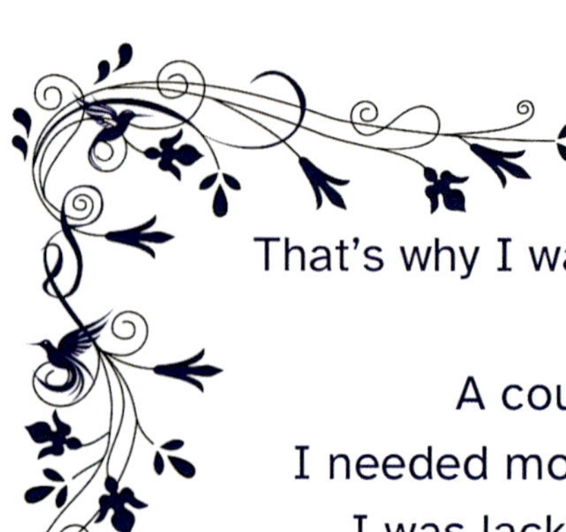

That's why I want to tell you **MY STORY**.

A couple of years ago,
I needed motivation **DESPERATELY**.
I was lacking focus and drive to
achieve any of my goals.

Without a **private** place
to display my vision board
(a vital tool for motivation and focus)
I searched for better options.
I needed MORE.
I needed something that I could
look at all day long to **sustain my focus**.

Therefore, I created a "pocket" version
that I could carry with me
and **hold** in my hands.

I wrote down my essential affirmations
and added inspiring quotes,
scriptures, and pictures,
that were **personal** to me,
that would help me **stay motivated**.

I would read them **every morning**
before getting out of bed.
(Honestly, some days it's the only thing
that got me out of bed and kept me positive.)

In moments of self-doubt and anxiety,
I would take out my pocket vision and
remind myself of my **WORTH** and **dreams**.

It was the **ACTION** of reading **my**
personal statements that helped me the most.

The result was an increased sense of focus
and determination that helped me
become my **BEST SELF**.

My mood throughout the day lifted
and my **ENERGY** soared!

My wish for you is to have the increased sense of
SELF-LOVE that I felt.

I am worthy.

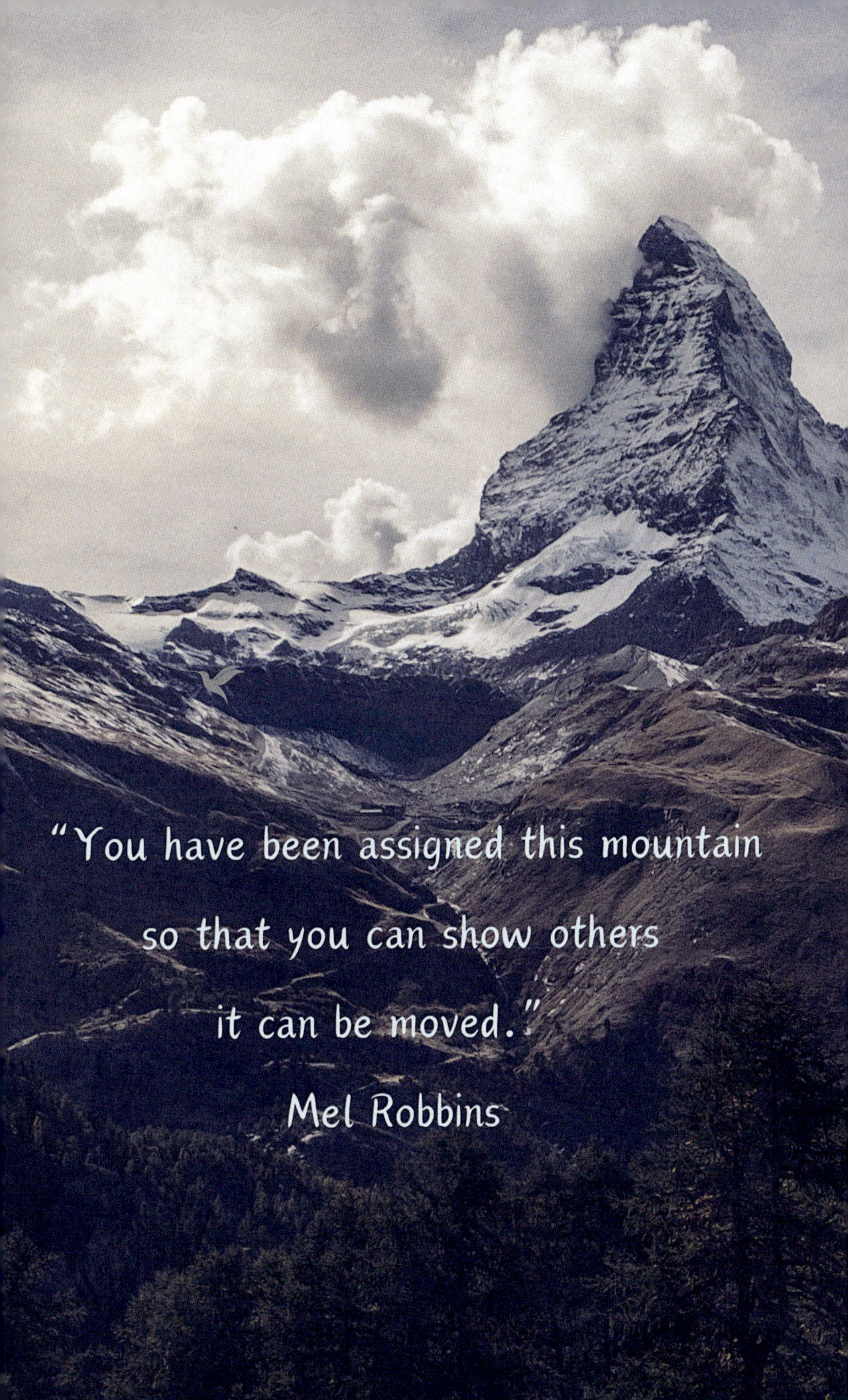

"You have been assigned this mountain
so that you can show others
it can be moved."
Mel Robbins

Golden Rules
How to get the most out of your Pocket Vision

Hey you! Yes, I am talking to you!

Today, we're going to smash some goals and feel **AMAZING** while doing it!

Let's start with some visually stunning inspiration -go ahead and paste or draw some images in here that light your **fire** and get your **heart pumping**. Paste some pictures of your **HAPPIEST** moments to make you smile when you need a boost.

Now, let's talk about the amazing person that you are.

Don't hold back, my friend!

Write some **affirmations**
that make you **feel** like the
wonderful, capable person that you are.

Speak to yourself in a **positive** and **loving**
tone, because you deserve all the
love and goodness in the world.

Let's get serious and write some
BOLD statements in the **present** tense
that make your heart race
with **EXCITEMENT**!

Start and end each day
saying these pages **OUT LOUD**!

Ditch the phone scrolling and
scroll through these pages giving you
ENERGY, CONFIDENCE AND JOY!

Why Pocket Vision?
Let's Start here,
Repeat after me:

I am **WORTHY** of loving myself.
Reading these pages will uplift how I feel.
How I feel influences everyone around me.
Working on myself is the most **LOVING**
thing I can do for other people.
Let's Do This!

Don't forget to snap some pictures
and TAG us so we can see your progress.
We want to
CONGRATULATE
you on your wins!
We are on your TEAM!
Confidence, here we come!

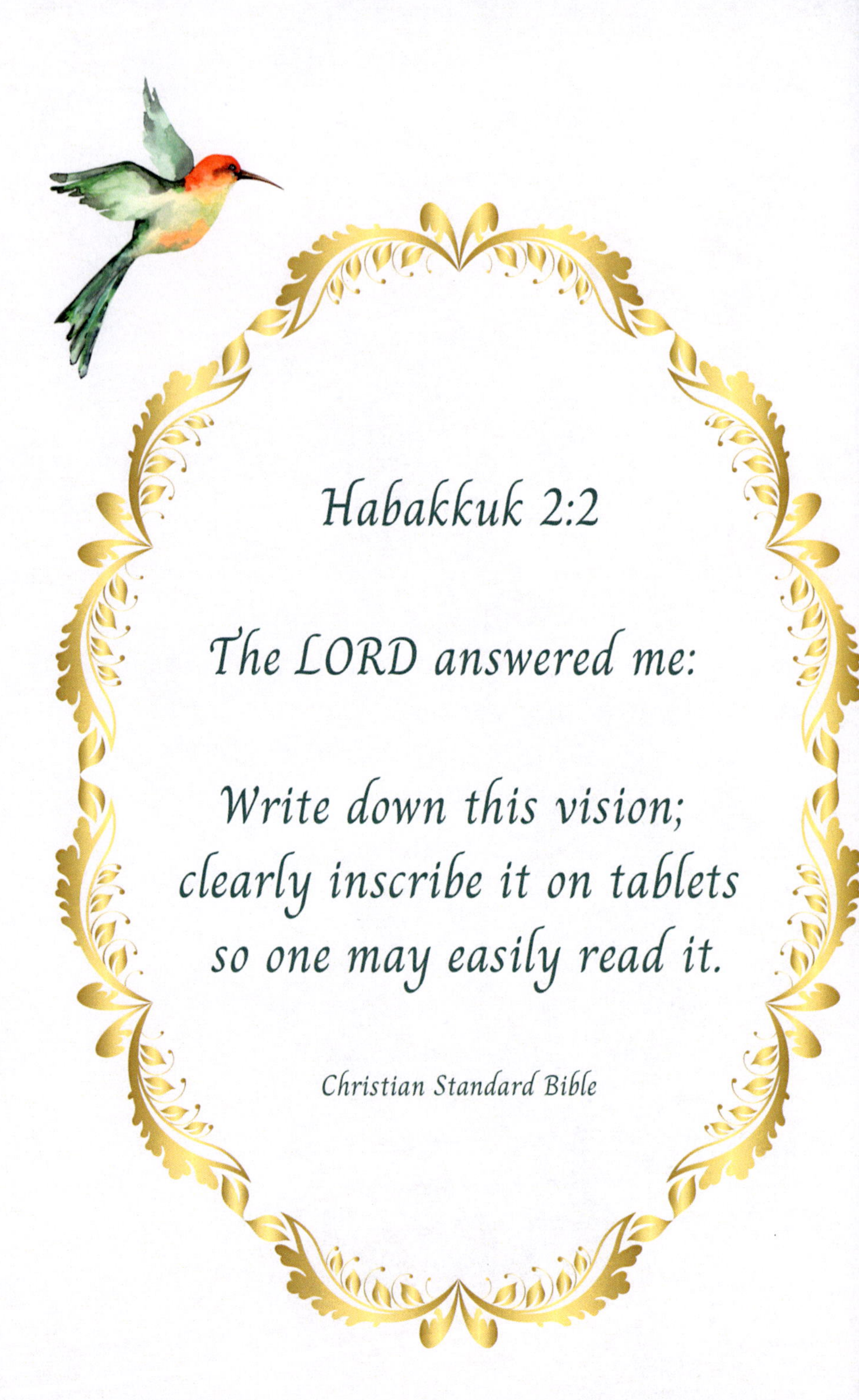

Habakkuk 2:2

The LORD answered me:

Write down this vision;
clearly inscribe it on tablets
so one may easily read it.

Christian Standard Bible

Here are the 7 sections
to EXPRESS yourself.

Fanatical- All about You!

Faith- What do you Believe?

Family- Who do you Love?

Friends- Who is your Village?

Fitness-Your Body and your Mind!

Finance- What is your Calling?

Fun- How do you get Energized?

Now Go, explore it, read it daily
and watch your world change!

Are you excited? **I am EXCITED**!

The **ADVENTURE** begins NOW!

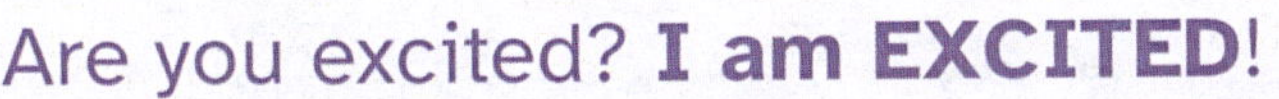

Grass is not greener
on the other side,
Grass is greener
where you water it.

I was born to do this!

Hummingbirds
Who knew?

Flitting into our lives, hummingbirds make you take **NOTICE** of them.

They bring joy and an instant **SMILE**. They pack a **POWERFUL** punch of hope and good vibes.

In fact, spotting one is a symbol that tough times are **behind** you, and **exciting new adventures** are on the horizon!

Hummingbirds will **LIFT** your spirits and release any lingering sadness, reminding you of your inner strength and resilience.

And boy, do they have a pep talk for you!
Patience, hope, and perseverance
are their mantras, **cheering** you on to
chase your dreams fearlessly.

These feathered friends are a
symbol of good luck, love, and beauty,
and are the perfect teachers for **gratitude**.
They are a reminder of healing and
letting go of grief and sadness.

They **INSPIR**E us to cherish the present,
and not sweat the small stuff.
Whenever you feel low, hummingbirds
remind you that **you're not alone**,
and that you are LOVED
UNCONDITIONALLY by your **Creator**.

Inspiring **adaptability** and **freedom**,
they fly forward, backward, up, down
and they hover.

Hummingbirds encourage us to **let go** of
negativity and embrace joy and positivity.
A sign of **good news** from Heaven,
they come when you mourn or feel lost.

My wish for you is to **no longer feel lost**
while reading your Pocket Vision
and to be **ENCOURAGED**
when you see a hummingbird.

(I have **hidden** hummingbirds on most
pages, I hope they make you smile.)

"Remember, your ears can hear you."
Amy Marie Tucker

I love Me.

Fanatical

Be your biggest Fan!

Being a superfan means you're all in,
with a heart full of passion
and a twinkle in your eye.

**The most important fan club to join
is the one for yourself!**

But first, you have to know who you are.

Take a moment to reflect and ask yourself:

"Do I really know the fabulous person I am?"

You are the **STAR** of your story,
and the best thing you can do is
SHINE BRIGHT by loving yourself!

Step one:

Get to know yourself inside and out.
Let's find out who you are!
Work on your vision for your life.

Step two:

Now, let's get creative!

Write down positive affirmations
and add some sparkle
by pasting or drawing uplifting pictures
that represent you in the present tense.

**Because, my friend,
you're worth celebrating!**

Powerful Examples to Kick-Start Your Self-Love Journey

I am a warrior!

I am adored and cherished!

I am a stunning masterpiece!

I am surrounded by love and support!

I give myself grace when I need it.

DONT' FORGET:
RESPECTING your own boundaries
is a form of self-love.
So, set those **BOUNDARIES,**
take care of yourself, and bask in the
glow of your own **AWESOMENESS**!

I AM protected.
I am a warrior
I am a survivor

Ephesians 6:13-17

13 Therefore put on the full armor of God, so that when the day of evil comes, you may be able to stand your ground, and after you have done everything, to stand. 14 Stand firm then, with the belt of truth buckled around your waist, with the breastplate of righteousness in place, 15 and with your feet fitted with the readiness that comes from the gospel of peace.

16 In addition to all this, take up the shield of faith, with which you can extinguish all the flaming arrows of the evil one.

17 Take the helmet of salvation and the sword of the Spirit, which is the word of God. NIV

If God is for me, who can be against me?
He hears my SOS & will send out an army
to find me in the middle of the darkest
night. ♥ Lauren Daigle.
He created me for something specific!

I am a super hero!

I can do anything I set my mind to.

★ Free

★ Confident

★ Kind

★ Authentic

★ Honest

I am independent.

I AM...

 Creative

 Fun + Funny

 His

 Loved

 Cherished by God.

"Reminder… Your body is listening to everything your mind is saying."
Dr. Mindy Pelz

I am extraordinary.

I am lovable.

I AM Enough

I am capable.
I am loveable.
He hides me 'neath His wings
He has a plan for my life.
He directs my steps.

I AM
Enough

I love who I am and who I am becoming!

Today is MY day!

I am taking action right now and I am facing today

with happiness and energy!

"I KNOW which team I am on,
and know THAT team wins."
Dr. Amanda Krueger

"Sometimes the bravest and most important thing
you can do is just show up."
Brene Brown

God has NEVER
failed me!

Faith

Share Your Heart's Voice

What sets your
soul on fire?

Do you know what you
stand for and
believe in?

This is the space to
shout it out loud!

Declare your passions,
your beliefs, your truth!

What ignites your heart
and fuels your spirit?

It's time to be heard!

God will provide.

Examples of
Faith-Fueled Phrases

I believe in my abilities
to make a difference.

My faith is a solid
foundation for
all that I do.

I know that even when
things get tough,
God's got my back.

My faith gives me the
courage and resilience
to tackle any obstacle.

Hebrews 11:1

Faith shows the reality
of what we hope for;
it is the evidence
of things
we cannot
see.

NLT

I am forgiven!

I BELIEVE

I make TIME for the things that MATTER the most.

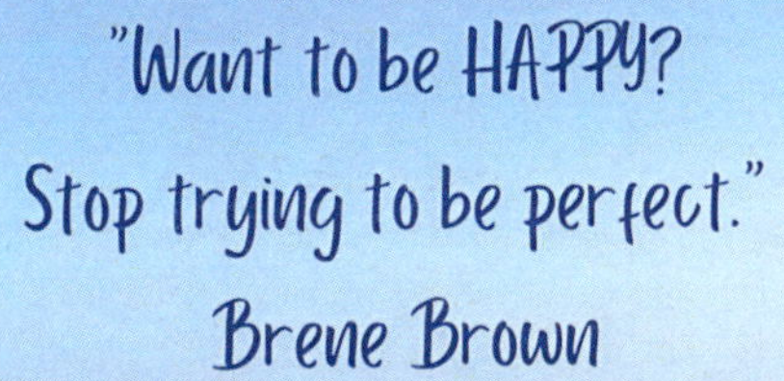
"Want to be HAPPY?
Stop trying to be perfect."
Brene Brown

I am happy!

Faith

I am loved.

I have good boundaries.
My boundaries are a reflection of my
self-respect and self-love.

I am Grateful!

I love my life!

Never, EVER, let your mood
dictate what you do.

I am BRAVE!

Now Go For the Gold!!

I am starting new traditions
that bring me joy!

"FAMILY IS NOT AN IMPORTANT THING.

IT'S EVERYTHING."

MICHAEL J. FOX

Tell us about your home team!

Any furry friends or awesome cousins?

What does family mean to you?

Who holds you together when you are broken?

Who do you love unconditionally?

Who loves you unconditionally?

Examples of Things
That Make Life Sweeter

Hanging out with my family is my happy place!

My furry buddy and I love exploring outdoors.

Nothing beats cozying up with a purring ball of fur.

My grandkids light up my world like fireworks!

When my sister is around,
adventure is never far behind.

I am in a happy fulfilling relationship.

PSALM 133:1

HOW GOOD AND PLEASANT

IT IS WHEN GOD'S

PEOPLE LIVE

TOGETHER

IN UNITY!

NIV

family

I am grateful for my family.

MY DOG IS NOT MY PET.
MY DOG IS FAMILY.

I am adored.

I am jumping with joy!

"Work hard at your job
and you can make a LIVING.
Work hard on yourself
and you can make a FORTUNE."
Jim Rohn

I am joyful.

My past is not a reflection of my future.

I am a clean slate.

I am Beautiful!

"My goals make demands of me."
Amy Marie Tucker

I make time for what's important.

{ Friends }

**This is your village,
the family you get to pick.**

If you're in a tight spot, who you gonna call?
Ghostbusters! ...Just kidding!

But seriously, who is your go-to for help?

Here's a fun idea:
Print and stick some pictures of your tribe...
those who you can count on,
your own personal village.

I enjoy my life.

Examples of Expressing Gratitude and Building Connections

I am comfortable being my true self
around my friends.

I know I can always rely on them,
even in the middle of the night if
I'm stranded on the highway.

By joining small groups,
I am connecting with new people
and I expand my social circle.

I am grateful for all the wonderful things
in my life that bring me joy and fulfillment.

Ecclesiastes 4:9

Two people are
better off than one,
for they can help
each other succeed.

NLT

I am kind to myself,
my family, my friends, and my world.

I CHOOSE MY DESTINY.

I am blessed.

I attract positive people into my life.

I can rely on my friends for emotional support.

I can be myself with my friends.

I have friends who know the real me.

I am not alone!

There is only ONE time to start
and that time is NOW!

I am unique.

I was born to fly.

I am Important!

Do not just WISH on stars,
Reach for them!

I am at peace.

"Keep your face always toward the sunshine –
and shadows will fall behind you."
Walt Whitman

I love my body!

How do you show love and TLC for your mind and your body?

Cozy up reading a book.

Get some sunshine by a pool.

Kayak or relax in a hammock.

Swing your troubles away at the golf course.

Exercise your brain and body
with ping pong or pickleball!

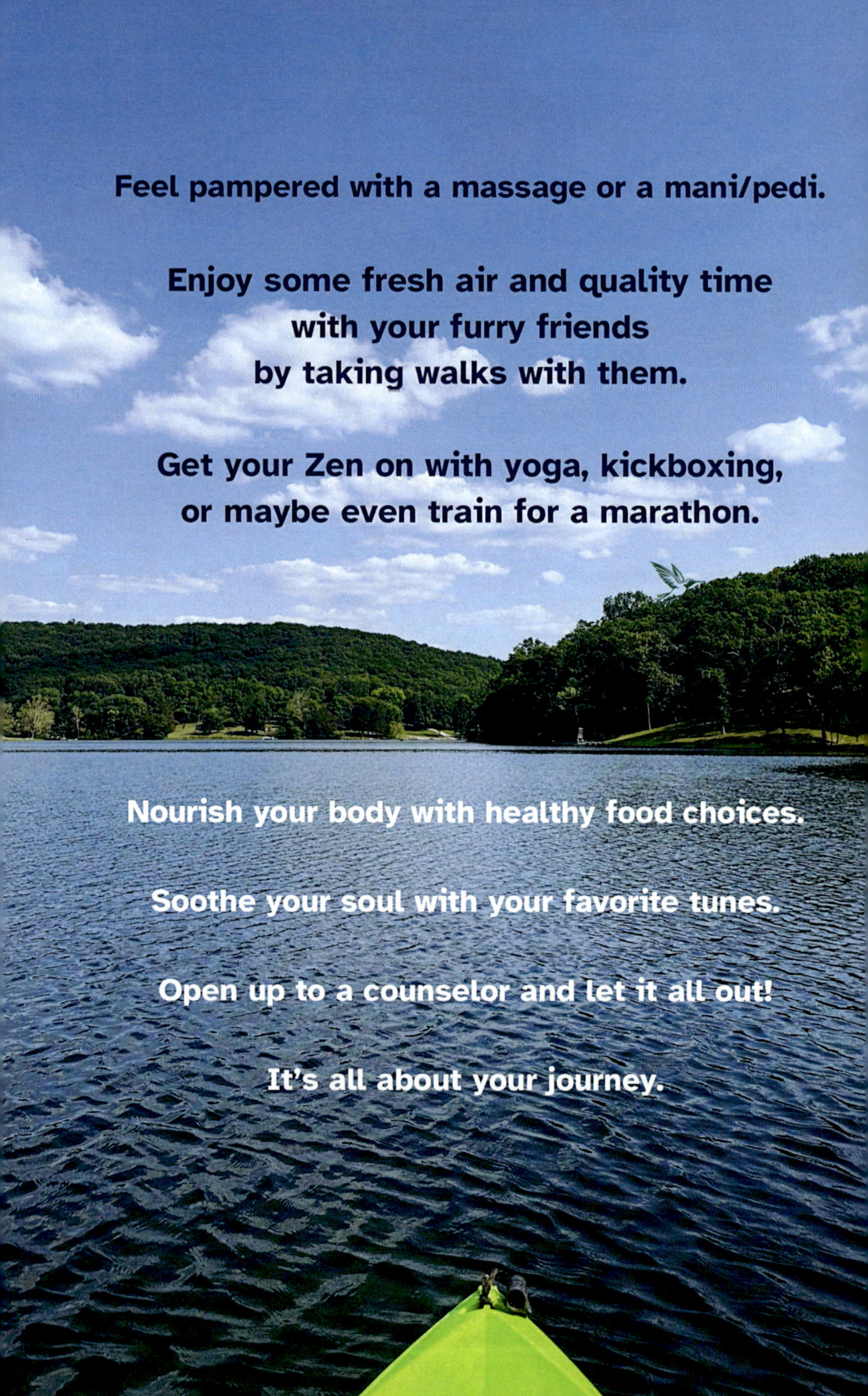

Feel pampered with a massage or a mani/pedi.

Enjoy some fresh air and quality time
with your furry friends
by taking walks with them.

Get your Zen on with yoga, kickboxing,
or maybe even train for a marathon.

Nourish your body with healthy food choices.

Soothe your soul with your favorite tunes.

Open up to a counselor and let it all out!

It's all about your journey.

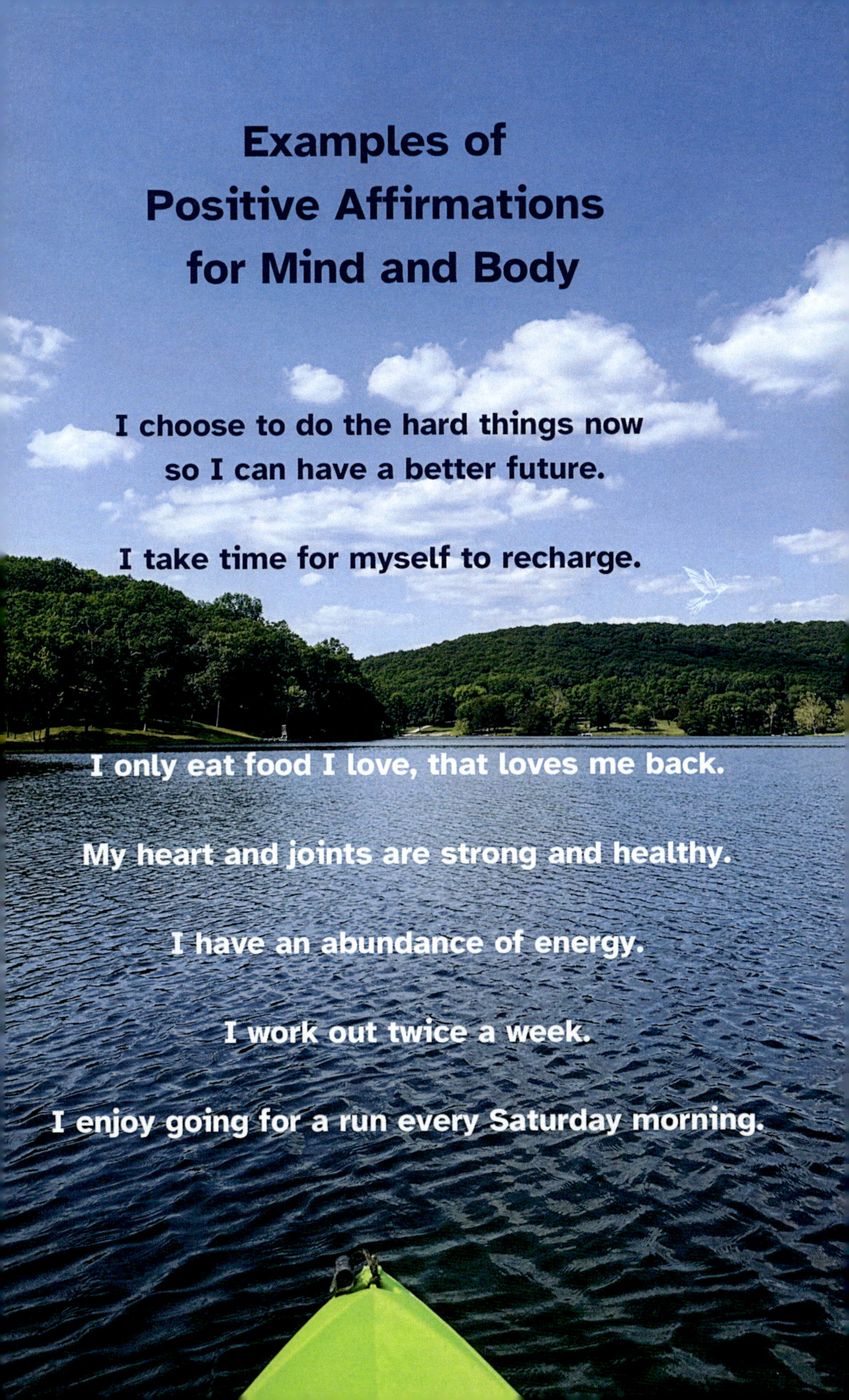

Examples of
Positive Affirmations
for Mind and Body

I choose to do the hard things now
so I can have a better future.

I take time for myself to recharge.

I only eat food I love, that loves me back.

My heart and joints are strong and healthy.

I have an abundance of energy.

I work out twice a week.

I enjoy going for a run every Saturday morning.

3 JOHN 1:2

DEAR FRIEND,

I HOPE

ALL IS WELL

WITH YOU

AND THAT

YOU ARE AS

HEALTHY

IN BODY

AS YOU ARE

STRONG

IN SPIRIT.

NLT

SOMETIMES
BEING
WITH YOUR
BEST FRIEND
IS ALL THE
THERAPY YOU
NEED.

I AM PROUD OF MYSELF!

"LOVE FOOD THAT LOVES YOU BACK."
DR. DANIEL AMEN

I am energized.

If them not choosing you
forced you to finally choose yourself,
YOU WIN.

I choose me.

SHINE
BRIGHT

I make healthy choices!

explore the world

I AM SMART AND CAPABLE.

I am everything
I need to be
to accomplish my goals.

"No matter how many
mistakes you make
or how slow you progress,
you are still way ahead
of everyone
who isn't trying."

Tony Robbins

I do what I love!

**Welcome to the section of
BIG dreams and Vision Planning!**

We're talking about work and income goals,
and setting your intentions with
specific affirmations.

So, let's get imaginative
and craft some detailed,
exciting goals
that will help you
live your BEST life!

**Make a plan... then make it BIGGER.
Reach for the STARS!**

Examples of How to INVEST in Your Daily Life

I spring out of bed each morning, ready to take on the day!

I strut my stuff, knowing I'm crushing my goals!

I'm on a mission to be debt-free and I'm slaying it!

I'm hustling hard to secure my dream home and biz!

I'm putting my nose to the grindstone to earn my degree!

I am generous.

I'm chasing my passion, working to score a job I adore!

Every day, I take purposeful action, living my best life!

I'm building my retirement fund like a boss!

Jeremiah 29:11

For I know the plans I have for you
—this is the LORD's declaration—
plans for your well-being, not for disaster,
to give you a future and a hope.

Christian Standard Bible

• I HAVE •
NO REGRETS

I tackle the hardest things first.

I have a plan in place
to accomplish my dreams.

"You do not rise to the level of your goals.
You fall to the level of your systems."
James Clear

I have complete faith.

"You are ONE decision away from a completely different life."
Mel Robbins
FINISH

I am appreciated.

"Comparison is the thief of joy."
Theodore Roosevelt

I WORK TOWARDS
WHAT MATTERS TO ME.

I FIGHT FOR WHAT I WANT.

"It is not too late
to do
what you want
to do
—if you stop
waiting
for the time
to be right."

James
Clear

Eat dessert FIRST.

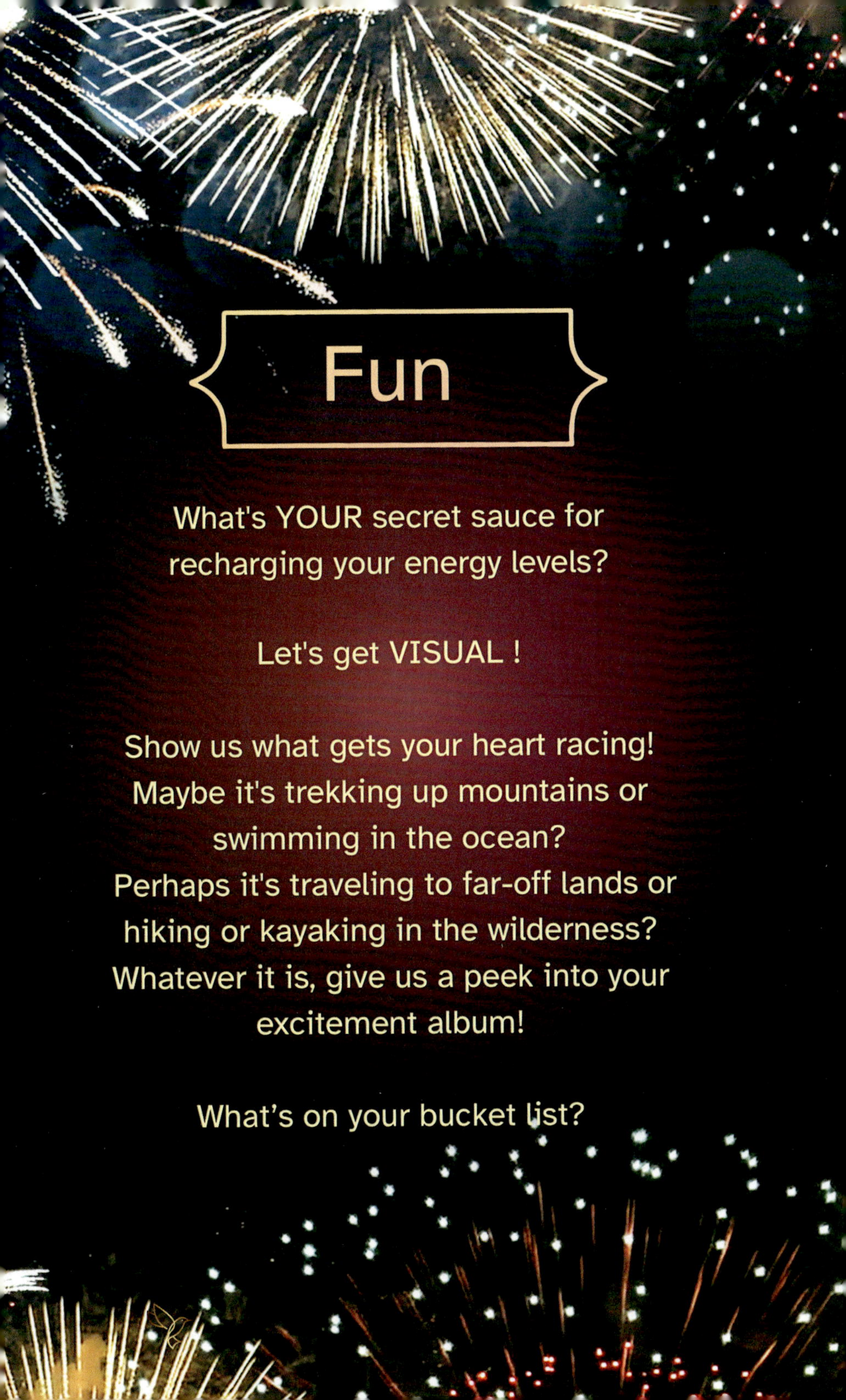

Fun

What's YOUR secret sauce for recharging your energy levels?

Let's get VISUAL !

Show us what gets your heart racing!
Maybe it's trekking up mountains or swimming in the ocean?
Perhaps it's traveling to far-off lands or hiking or kayaking in the wilderness?
Whatever it is, give us a peek into your excitement album!

What's on your bucket list?

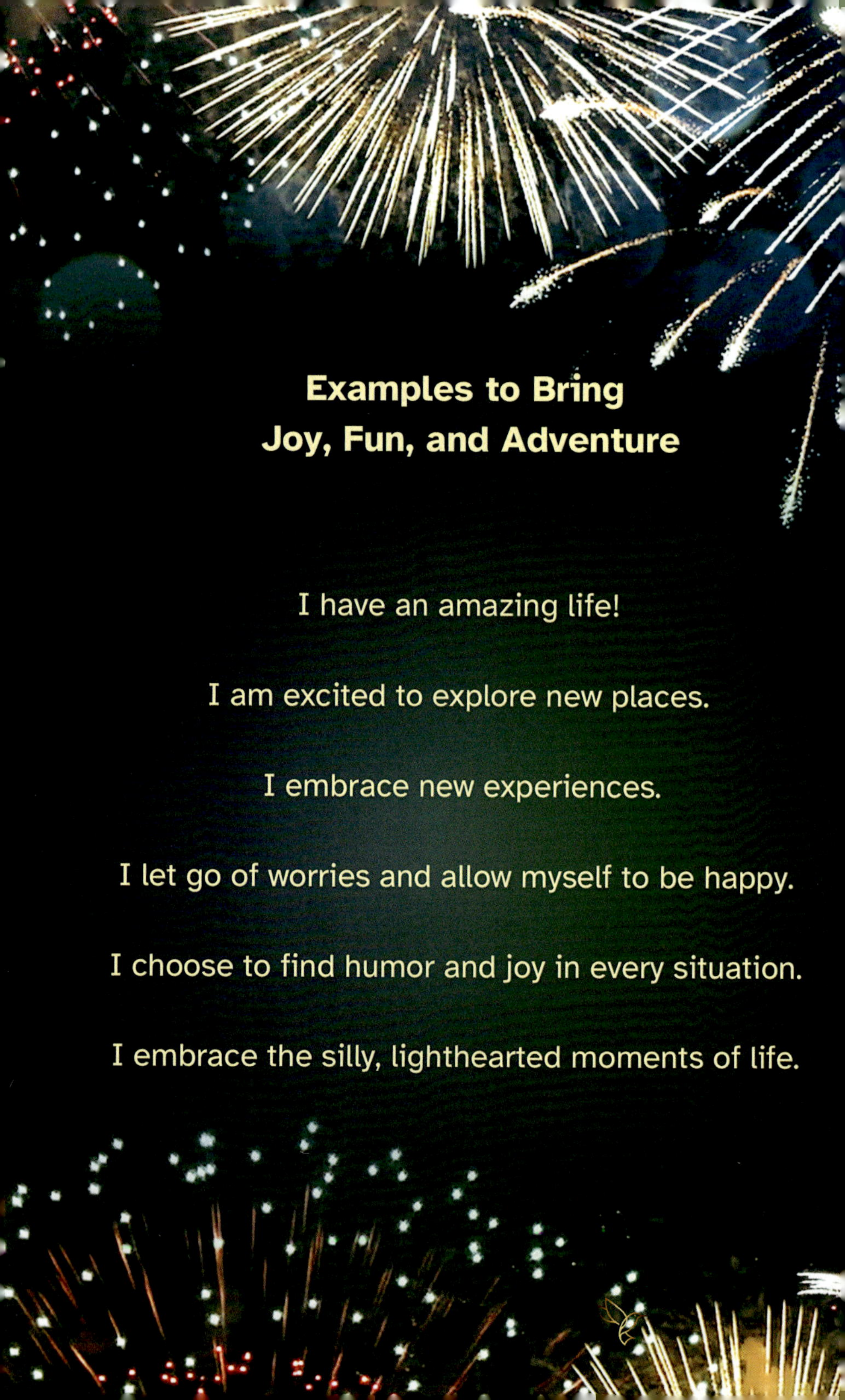

Examples to Bring
Joy, Fun, and Adventure

I have an amazing life!

I am excited to explore new places.

I embrace new experiences.

I let go of worries and allow myself to be happy.

I choose to find humor and joy in every situation.

I embrace the silly, lighthearted moments of life.

Hey Friend....
What gets you
up in the morning?

ACKERMA

Ecclesiastes 8:15

So I recommend having

FUN

because there is nothing better

for people in this world

than to eat, drink, and enjoy life.

That way they will experience some

HAPPINESS

along with all the hard work

God gives them under the sun.

NLT

"Right foot, left foot...rinse and repeat."
Dr. Amanda Krueger

I walk in faith.

Time will pass whether you do this or not.

Don't look back and wish you had already started.

I WAS BORN TO STAND OUT!

I am resilient.

"You cannot change your destination overnight,
but you can change your direction overnight."
Jim Rohn

I dance when it rains!

I am adventurous.

I BUILD MY LIFE
WITH MY WORDS AND MY ACTIONS.

"My love for you will ever flow, like water down a tater row."

Let's GO!
BEGIN
GO
READ
LEARN
Get lost
in the right
direction

REMINDERS

Monday

Tuesday

Wednesday

Thursday

Friday

Saturday

Sunday

Daily

GOOD MORNING GORGEOUS!
____
Read this book out loud

- [ ] ______________________
- [ ] ______________________
- [ ] ______________________
- [ ] ______________________
- [ ] ______________________
- [ ] ______________________
- [ ] ______________________
- [ ] ______________________
- [ ] ______________________
- [ ] ______________________
- [ ] WHAT WENT WELL TODAY?
____

I AM PROUD OF ME TODAY!

Notes

____
____
____
____
____
____
____
____
____

I read
my affirmations
daily
to empower,
express and
show love
to my new self!

"Everything you need to be
great
is already inside you.
Stop waiting
for someone or something
to light the fire.
You have the match."
Darren Hardy

I am kind to my future self.

Bonus Section

Letter to YOU from your FUTURE SELF

How to Write your letter:

Decide on a future date
that you are writing from.

This gives you a way to
reflect on your life right
now and consider how it
will appear for
example 3 to 5 years
in the future.

Use your tone of voice,
so it sounds like you are
talking to yourself.

I am seen.

Talk to yourself about:

Work, Money, Self, Relationship, Spiritual, Faith, Family, Friends, Fun, Gratitude

Begin with
Dear (your name),
It is
(date in the future)
and then write your vision, and then...
make it bigger!

Use the next several pages to be inspired and record that letter for you to read back to yourself at that future date.

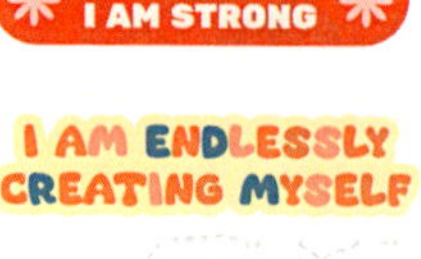

I am proud
of myself!

• I am •
CONFIDENT

YOUR OPINION
OF ME
DOESN'T DEFINE
WHO I AM

You
DON'T
NEED TO BE
AN EXPERT
TO DO
SOMETHING
GREAT

I am
SMART

MINDSET
IS
EVERYTHING

I AM STRONG
I AM CAPABLE
I AM RESILIENT

I'M WORTHY
OF LOVE
AND HAPPINESS

I ADD VALUE
TO THE
WORLD

Change your **Words**
Change your **Life**

Shout out to **Coach Dan Keller**
who reminded me that writing a letter to you from
your future self can be so impactful.

**Thanks to the author's,
motivational speakers, and coaches,
your quotes have impacted and inspired me.
I hope the readers enjoy them as much as I do.**

With LOVE and GRATITUDE

HUGE Thanks to my son **Jacob Stanley**
for multiple photo contributions,
editing support and design consultation.

While we are shouting, BIG thanks to
my daughter **Carlee Stanley**
for having these hummingbirds created for me
from her long-time best friend Ellie Paisley
@ellie.paisley
(check out her artwork, it's amazing!)

Harvey the Great Dane in the photo
is her family, not her Dog.

Big BEAR HUGS for my son **Austin Stanley**
for the input, suggestions and multiple photos
from his recent honeymoon trip.

With LOTS OF LOVE
to the LIGHTS of my life
my grandkids,
Max, Hazel, and Haven.

"So, which one are you?"
Me, "Aren't you always to my right?"
Hahahahaha
(Amy and I looking at pictures growing up.)

Big shoutout to my amazing twin sister,
(Always the one to my right,
but does that make her *always* right? hmmm)

Amy Marie Tucker!
She can see the sparkle in me,
even when I can't quite see it myself.
She's my personal editor and my magic mirror, always
pushing me to grow with her "gentle" advice.
Amy went above and beyond to make this book shine,
giving it a spiffy, professional edge,
making me look like a pro!

(Maybe because what I do reflects on her too? Ha!)

That photo with her quote?
It was snapped from our wild adventure in Mexico
last year, and it holds a deep meaning for us.

It's a reminder that tomorrow is packed with potential
and to be kind to ourselves with what we say.

"Remember, your ears can hear you!"
Amy Marie Tucker

Please Subscribe and Follow us on Social Media

Instagram @michellemarieauthor
Facebook Michelle Marie Author
Pinterest Michelle Marie Author
for "pocket-sized" clip art ideas
www.michellemarieauthor.com

#pocketvision
#michellemarie
#hummingbirdsunite

Now I am asking for help with my Dream!!
Please help a girl out!
Post a picture of you reading your Pocket Vision and
tag me on any of my social media.

I will be **giving away** hummingbird window clings,
clip art, etc. to random winners.
I will DM/tag winners on social media.

Thanks as always for the support!
I appreciate you!

Look for our new books coming in 2024!

Voices of Children of DiVorce
It's time to be heard!
Grown children speak about
the affects of diVorce on their lives.

Voices of DiVorced,
DiVorce stories shared by Women
You are not alone!

(You will understand the unique spelling when you read the books.)

We want to hear from you!

Tell us your story! I am looking for more interviews for
divorced people and children of divorce.
Talk to us at
info@michellemarieauthor.com

Credits

Page 19: Robbins, Mel. 2017. The 5 Second Rule. Savio Republic. https://doi.org/https://www.goodreads.com/quotes/8754088-you-have-been-assigned-this-mountain-so-that-you-can.

Page 33: Langston, Ann Michelle Interviewed Tucker, Amy Marie. Dec. 2023

Page 43: Pelz, Mindy. " Reminder." Instagram. November 6, 2023. https://doi.org/https://www.instagram.com/dr.mindypelz/p/CzT-x7dqqVI/.

Page 50: Langston, Ann Michelle Interviewed Krueger, Dr. Amanda. Dec. 2023

Page 51; Brown, Brene. 2012. Daring Greatly. Avery. https://www.goodreads.com/quotes/6904216-sometimes-the-bravest-and-most-important-thing-you-can-do.

Page 63: Brown, Brene. 2010. The Gifts of Imperfection. Hazelden. https://www.cnn.com/2010/LIVING/11/01/give.up.perfection/index.html#:~:text=She%20is%20the%20author%20of,%22What%20will%20people%20think%3F%22.

Page 75:Fox, Michael J. "Family Is Not an Important Thing. It's Everything." Www.Imdb.Com. Michael J Fox Show, December 12, 2013. https://doi.org/https://www.imdb.com/name/nm0000150/bio/.t

Page 85: Rohn, Jim. " Work Hard at Your Job and You Can Make a Living. Work Hard on Yourself and You Can Make a Fortune." Facebook. September 11, 2014 https://doi.org/https://www.facebook.com/OfficialJimRohn/posts/10154545280230635.

Page 91: Langston, Ann Michelle Interviewed Tucker, Amy Marie. Dec. 2023

Page 111: Whitman, Walt. 2016. Walt Whitman Quotes...Vol. 20. The SECRET Libraries. https://www.goodreads.com/book/show/40668585-walt-whitman-quotesvol20from_search=true&from_srp=true&qid=98RvpKF1gW&rank=2.

Page 122: [Amen Clinics/ You Tube]. (2022, October 12). "Love Food That Loves You Back." [Video]. You Tube. https://www.youtube.com/watch?v=pPvZUtwZQP0

Page 131:: [Tony Robbins/ Facebook]. (2012, June 3). "No matter how many mistakes you make or how slow you progress, you are still way ahead of everyone who isn't trying." [Video]. Facebook https://www.facebook.com/TonyRobbins/posts/10150942540369060

Credits

Page 143: Clear, James. 2018. Atomic Habits. Avery. https://jamesclear.com/quotes/you-do-not-rise-to-the-level-of-your-goals-you-fall-to-the-level-of-your-systems.

Page 145: Robbins, Me. 2017. The 5 Second Rule. Savio Republic. https://doi.org/https://www.goodreads.com/quotes/8326073-you-are-one-decision-away-from-a-completely-different-life.

Page 147: Roosevelt, Theodore. 1962. Theodore Roosevelt's America: Selections from the Writings of the Oyster Bay Naturalist. The Natural HistoryLibrary.https://doi.org/https://www.goodreads.com/book/show/21410298-theodore-roosevelt-s-america?from_search=true&from_srp=true&qid=3CmAwujEOg&rank=1.

Page 151: Clear, James. ""It Is Not Too Late to Do what You Want to Do —If You Stop Waiting or the Time to Be Right"." Jamesclear.Com/Quote/Motivational. November 30, 2023. https://doi.org/https://jamesclear.com/quote/motivational.

Page 160: Langston, Ann Michelle Interviewed Krueger, Dr. Amanda. Dec. 2023

Page 165: Rohn, J. (2017, May 1). "You cannot change your destination overnight, but you can change your direction overnight.". RetrievedDecember 30, 2023, from https://www.facebook.com/OfficialJimRohn/posts/10158597000340635

Page 169: Langston, Ann Michelle Interviewed Bushong, Eileen Isabel Gaskins "Grandomother Beautiful". Dec. 2023

Page 175: Hardy, Darren . "Everything You Need to Be Great Is Already inside You. Stop Waiting forSomeone or Something to Light Your Fire. You Have the Match." Facebook. December 31, 2014. https://doi.org/https://www.facebook.com/DarrenHardyFan/posts/101529660059547287:0.

Photo Credits

Pages:26,27,32,33,45,58,59,74,75,76,77,98,99,114,115,116,117,124,125,150,151 169 Langston, A. (2023). Multiple images [Photograph]. Personal Michelle Marie.

Pages: 50,51,62,63,158,159:Stanley, A. (2023). Multiple images [Photograph]. Personal.

Pages: 54,55,56,57,82,168: Stanley, J. (2023). Multiple images [Photograph]. Personal.

Pages: 90,91,161: Amy, T. (2023). Multiple images [Photograph]. Personal.

Pages: 106,189: Paisley, E. (2023). Multiple images [Photograph]. Carlee Stanley. @ellie.paisley